Acetate Masters

for Worship Songs

Kevin Mayhew

First published in 1997 by
KEVIN MAYHEW LTD
Rattlesden Bury St Edmunds
Suffolk IP30 0SZ

ISBN 0 86209 936 6
Catalogue No 1385002

0 1 2 3 4 5 6 7 8 9

Front cover: *Sweeping red and yellow clouds at sunset*
Reproduced by courtesy of Tony Stone Images, London

Cover design by Graham Johnstone

Edited by David Gatward
Typesetting by Louise Hill
Printed and bound in Great Britain

Copyright Information

This book is designed for use by those churches and schools in the UK who possess a Christian Copyright Licensing (CCL) licence and must be used within the terms of that licence. Please ensure that each time you use a song it is entered on your Song Survey Worksheet to enable CCL to allocate the appropriate royalties.

We would like to remind churches and schools who do not possess a CCL licence that the use of these masters is illegal without first obtaining the written permission of the individual copyright holders whose details are given under each song. This stipulation also applies to those churches or schools who do possess a licence but wish to use these masters outside the terms of that licence.

If you would like to obtain a CCL licence or require further information about CCL, please contact them at the following address:

CCL (Europe) Ltd
PO Box 1339
Eastbourne
East Sussex
BN21 4YF

Tel: 01323 417711
Fax: 01323 417722

Most of the songs in this book will also be covered by Christian Copyright Licences in other countries. Please contact your local office for guidance.

United States & Canada:
CCL Inc
17201 NE Sacramento Street
Portland
Oregon 97230

New Zealand:
CCL Asia-Pacific Pty Ltd
PO Box 26405
Epsom
Auckland 3

Australia:
CCL Asia-Pacific Pty Ltd
PO Box 6644
Baulkham Hills Business Centre
New South Wales 2153

Southern Africa:
CCL Africa (Pty) Ltd
PO Box 2347
Durbanville 7551

Contents

All heaven declares
the glory of the risen Lord.
Who can compare
with the beauty of the Lord?
For ever he will be
the Lamb upon the throne.
I gladly bow the knee
and worship him alone.

I will proclaim
the glory of the risen Lord.
Who once was slain
to reconcile man to God.
For ever you will be
the Lamb upon the throne.
I gladly bow the knee
and worship you alone.

Noel Richards & Tricia Richards

Almighty God, we bring you praise
for your Son, the word of God,
by whose power the world was made,
by whose blood we are redeemed.
Morning star, the Father's glory,
we now worship and adore you;
In our hearts your light has risen;
Jesus, Lord, we worship you.

Austin Martin

And can it be that I should gain
an interest in the Saviour's blood?
Died he for me, who caused his pain?
For me, who him to death pursued?
Amazing love! how can it be
that thou, my God, shouldst die for me!

'Tis mystery all! The immortal dies:
who can explore his strange design?
In vain the first-born seraph tries
to sound the depths of love divine.
'Tis mercy all, let earth adore,
let angel minds inquire no more.

He left his Father's throne above,
so free, so infinite his grace;
emptied himself of all but love,
and bled for Adam's helpless race.
'Tis mercy all, immense and free;
for, O my God, it found out me!

Charles Wesley

CCL Licence No. _____

Long my imprisoned spirit lay
fast bound in sin and nature's night;
thine eye diffused a quickening ray
I woke, the dungeon flamed with light;
my chains fell off, my heart was free.
I rose, went forth, and followed thee.

No condemnation now I dread;
Jesus, and all in him, is mine!
Alive in him, my living head,
and clothed in righteousness divine,
bold I approach the eternal throne,
and claim the crown, through Christ, my own.

Charles Wesley

As the deer pants for the water
so my soul longs after you.
You alone are my heart's desire
and I long to worship you.

You alone are my strength, my shield,
to you alone may my spirit yield.
You alone are my heart's desire
and I long to worship you.

I want you more than gold or silver,
only you can satisfy.
You alone are the real joy-giver
and the apple of my eye.

You alone . . .

You're my friend and you are my brother
even though you are a King.
I love you more than any other,
so much more than anything.

You alone . . .

Martin Nystrom

CCL Licence No. _____

Be patient, be ready,
look up, the Lord is near.
Be faithful, be fruitful,
until the day that he appears.
Though all things are shaken
and hearts are filled with fear;
keep working, keep praying,
until his kingdom is here.

Deep in our hearts there's a cry,
as the Spirit and bride say:
'Come, Jesus, come, take your white horse
and ride through the heavens. Come!'
Deep in our hearts there's a cry,
as the Spirit and bride say:
'Come, Jesus, come, take your white horse
and ride through the heavens. Come!'

Graham Kendrick

By your side I would stay;
in your arms I would lay.
Jesus, lover of my soul,
nothing from you I withhold.

Lord, I love you and adore you;
what more can I say?
You cause my love to grow stronger
with every passing day.
Lord, I love you and adore you;
what more can I say?
You cause my love to grow stronger
with every passing day.

Noel Richards & Tricia Richards

Copyright © 1989 Kingsway's Thankyou Music, P.O. Box 75, Eastbourne,
East Sussex, BN23 6NW, U.K. Used by permission.

CCL Licence No. _____

Change my heart, O God, make it ever true,
change my heart, O God, may I be like you.
You are the potter, I am the clay,
mould me and make me, this is what I pray.
Change my heart, O God, make it ever true,
change my heart, O God, may I be like you.

Eddie Espinosa

Colours of day dawn into the mind,
the sun has come up, the night is behind.
Go down in the city, into the street,
and let's give the message to the people we meet.

So light up the fire and let the flame burn,
open the door, let Jesus return.
Take seeds of his Spirit, let the fruit grow,
tell the people of Jesus, let his love show.

Go through the park, on into the town;
the sun still shines on, it never goes down.
The light of the world is risen again;
the people of darkness are needing a friend.

So light up the fire . . .

Open your eyes, look into the sky,
the darkness has come, the sun came to die.
The evening drawn on, the sun disappears,
but Jesus is living, his Spirit is near.

So light up the fire . . .

Sue McClellan, John Paculabo & Keith Ryecroft

Copyright © 1974 Kingsway's Thankyou Music, P.O. Box 75, Eastbourne,
East Sussex, BN23 6NW, U.K. Used by permission.

Down the mountain the river flows,
and it brings refreshing wherever it goes.
Through the valleys and over the fields,
the river is rushing and the river is here.

The river of God
sets our feet a-dancing,
the river of God
fills our hearts with cheer,
the river of God
fills our mouths with laughter,
and we rejoice,
for the river is here!

The river of God is teeming with life,
and all who touch it can be revived,
and those who linger on this river's shore
will come back thirsting for more of the Lord.

The river of God . . .

Andy Park

Copyright © 1994 Mercy/Vineyard Publishing. Administered in the UK and Eire by Integrity's
Hosanna! Music, P.O. Box 101, Eastbourne, East Sussex, BN21 4SZ, UK.
All rights reserved. International copyright secured. Used by permission.

Up to the mountain we love to go,
to find the presence of the Lord.
Along the banks of the river we run,
we dance with laughter, giving praise to the Son.

The river of God
sets our feet a-dancing,
the river of God
fills our hearts with cheer,
the river of God
fills our mouths with laughter,
and we rejoice,
for the river is here!

Andy Park

Copyright © 1994 Mercy/Vineyard Publishing. Administered in the UK and Eire by Integrity's Hosanna! Music, P.O. Box 101, Eastbourne, East Sussex, BN21 4SZ, UK. All rights reserved. International copyright secured. Used by permission.

CCL Licence No. _____

Fairest Lord Jesus,
Lord of all creation,
Jesus, of God and man the Son;
you will I cherish,
you will I honour,
you are my soul's delight and crown.

Fair are the rivers,
meadows and forests,
clothed in the fresh green robes of spring;
Jesus is fairer,
Jesus is purer,
he makes the saddest heart to sing.

Fair is the sunrise;
starlight and moonlight
spreading their glory across the sky;
Jesus shines brighter,
Jesus shines clearer
than all the heavenly host on high.

Lilian Stevenson

All fairest beauty,
heavenly and earthly,
Jesus, my Lord, in you I see;
none can be nearer,
fairer or dearer
than you, my Saviour, are to me.

Lilian Stevenson

Faithful one, so unchanging,
ageless one, you're my rock of peace.
Lord of all, I depend on you,
I call out to you again and again.
I call out to you again and again.

You are my rock in times of trouble.
You lift me up when I fall down.
All through the storm your love
is the anchor, my hope is in you alone.

Brian Doerksen

Father, I place into your hands
the things I cannot do.
Father, I place into your hands
the things that I've been through.
Father, I place into your hands
the way that I should go
for I know I always can trust you.

Father, I place into your hands
my friends and family.
Father, I place into your hands
the things that trouble me.
Father, I place into your hands
the person I would be
for I know I always can trust you.

Jenny Hewer

Father, we love to see your face,
we love to hear your voice.
Father, we love to sing your praise
and in your name rejoice.
Father, we love to walk with you
and in your presence rest,
for we know we always can trust you.

Father, I want to be with you
and do the things you do.
Father, I want to speak the words
that you are speaking too.
Father, I want to love the ones
that you will draw to you,
for I know that I am one with you.

Jenny Hewer

From heav'n you came, helpless babe,
entered our world, your glory veiled;
not to be served but to serve,
and give your life that we might live.

This is our God, the Servant King,
he calls us now to follow him,
to bring our lives as a daily offering
of worship to the Servant King.

There in the garden of tears,
my heavy load he chose to bear;
his heart with sorrow was torn.
'Yet not my will but yours,' he said.

This is our God . . .

Come see his hands and his feet,
the scars that speak of sacrifice,
hands that flung stars into space
to cruel nails surrendered.

This is our God . . .

Graham Kendrick

So let us learn how to serve,
and in our lives enthrone him;
each other's needs to prefer,
for it is Christ we're serving.

This is our God, the Servant King,
he calls us now to follow him,
to bring our lives as a daily offering
of worship to the Servant King.

Graham Kendrick

God is good, we sing and shout it,
God is good, we celebrate.
God is good, no more we doubt it,
God is good, we know it's true.

And when I think of his love for me,
my heart fills with praise
and I feel like dancing.
For in his heart there is room for me
and I run with arms opened wide.

(Last time)
God is good, we sing and shout it,
God is good, we celebrate.
God is good, no more we doubt it,
God is good, we know it's true. Hey!

Graham Kendrick

He has risen, he has risen,
he has risen, Jesus is alive.

When the life flowed from his body,
seemed like Jesus' mission failed.
But his sacrifice accomplished,
vict'ry over sin and hell.

He has risen . . .

In the grave God did not leave him,
for his body to decay;
raised to life, the great awakening,
Satan's power he overcame.

He has risen . . .

If there were no resurrection,
we ourselves could not be raised;
but the Son of God is living,
so our hope is not in vain.

He has risen . . .

Gerald Coates, Noel Richards & Tricia Richards

**Copyright © 1993 Kingsways Thankyou Music, P.O. Box 75, Eastbourne,
East Sussex, BN23 6NW, U.K. Used by permission.**

CCL Licence No. _____

When the Lord rides out of heaven,
mighty angels at his side,
they will sound the final trumpet,
from the grave we shall arise.

He has risen, he has risen,
he has risen, Jesus is alive.

He has given life immortal,
we shall see him face to face;
through eternity we'll praise him,
Christ, the champion of our faith.

He has risen . . .

Gerald Coates, Noel Richards & Tricia Richards

CCL Licence No. _____

(Men)	Hold me, Lord,
(Women)	hold me, Lord,
(Men)	in your arms,
(Women)	in your arms,
(Men)	fill me, Lord
(Women)	fill me, Lord
(All)	with your Spirit.

(Men)	Touch my heart,
(Women)	touch my heart,
(Men)	with your love,
(Women)	with your love,
(Men)	let my life,
(Women)	let my life,
(All)	glorify your name.
	Singing alleluia, singing alleluia,
	singing alleluia, singing alleluia.

(Men)	Alleluia,
(Women)	alleluia,
(Men)	allelu,
(Women)	allelu,
(Men)	alleluia,
(Women)	alleluia,
(Men)	allelu,
(Women)	allelu.

Danny Daniels

Hosanna, hosanna,
hosanna in the highest!
Hosanna, hosanna,
hosanna in the highest!
Lord, we lift up your name
with hearts full of praise;
be exalted, O Lord my God!
Hosanna in the highest!

Glory, glory,
glory to the King of kings!
Glory, glory,
glory to the King of kings!
Lord, we lift up your name
with hearts full of praise;
be exalted, O Lord, my God!
Glory to the King of kings!

Carl Tuttle

CCL Licence No. _____

I just want to praise you;
lift my hands and say 'I love you'.
You are everything to me,
and I exalt your holy name on high.

I just want to praise you;
lift my hands and say 'I love you'.
You are everything to me,
and I exalt your holy name;
I exalt your holy name,
I exalt your holy name on high.

Arthur Tannous

I lift my eyes up to the mountains,
where does my help come from?
My help comes from you, maker of heaven,
creator of the earth.
O how I need you, Lord,
you are my only hope;
you're my only prayer.
So I will wait for you
to come and rescue me,
come and give me life.

Brian Doerksen

I sing a simple song of love
to my Saviour, to my Jesus.
I'm grateful for the things you've done,
my loving Saviour, O precious Jesus.
My heart is glad that you've called me your own,
there's no place I'd rather be
than in your arms of love,
in your arms of love,
holding me still,
holding me near,
in your arms of love.

Last time:

holding me still,
holding me near,
holding me still,
holding me near,
holding me still,
holding me near
in your arms of love.

Craig Musseau

I will enter his gates with thanksgiving in my heart,
I will enter his courts with praise,
I will say this is the day that the Lord has made,
I will rejoice for he has made me glad.

He has made me glad,
he has made me glad,
I will rejoice for he has made me glad.
He has made me glad,
he has made me glad,
I will rejoice for he has made me glad.

Leona von Brethorst

Copyright © 1976 Maranatha! Music. Administered by CopyCare,
P.O. Box 77, Hailsham, BN27 3EF, U.K. Used by permission.

CCL Licence No. _____

In heavenly armour
we'll enter the land,
the battle belongs to the Lord.
No weapon that's fashioned
against us will stand,
the battle belongs to the Lord.

And we sing glory, honour,
power and strength to the Lord,
we sing glory, honour,
power and strength to the Lord.

When the power of darkness
comes in like a flood,
the battle belongs to the Lord.
He'll raise up a standard,
the power of his blood,
the battle belongs to the Lord.

And we sing . . .

Jamie Owens-Collins

CCL Licence No. _____

When your enemy presses in hard,
do not fear,
the battle belongs to the Lord.
Take courage my friend,
your redemption is near
the battle belongs to the Lord.

And we sing glory, honour,
power and strength to the Lord,
we sing glory, honour,
power and strength to the Lord.

Jamie Owens-Collins

Jesus, stand among us
at the meeting of our lives,
be our sweet agreement
at the meeting of our eyes;

O, Jesus, we love you,
so we gather here,
join our hearts in unity
and take away our fear.

So to you we're gathering
out of each and every land,
Christ the love between us
at the joining of our hands;

O, Jesus, we love you . . .

(Optional verse for communion:)

Jesus, stand among us
at the breaking of the bread,
join us as one body
as we worship you, our Head.

O, Jesus, we love you . . .

Graham Kendrick

CCL Licence No. _____

Jesus, we celebrate your victory;
Jesus, we revel in your love.
Jesus, we rejoice, you've set us free;
Jesus, your death has brought us life.

It was for freedom that Christ has set us free,
no longer to be subject to a yoke of slavery;
so we're rejoicing in God's victory,
our hearts responding to his love.

Jesus, we celebrate your victory . . .

His Spirit in us releases us from fear,
the way to him is open, with boldness we draw near.
And in his presence our problems disappear;
Our hearts responding to his love.

Jesus, we celebrate your victory . . .

John Gibson

Led like a lamb
to the slaughter
in silence and shame,
there on your back
you carried a world
of violence and pain:
bleeding, dying,
bleeding, dying.

You're alive, you're alive,
you have risen!
Alleluia!
And the power and the glory
is given,
alleluia,
Jesus, to you.

At break of dawn,
poor Mary,
still weeping she came,
when through her grief
she heard your voice
now speaking her name:
Mary, Master,
Mary, Master.

Graham Kendrick

You're alive, you're alive,
you have risen!
Alleluia!
And the power and the glory
is given,
alleluia,
Jesus, to you.

At the right hand
of the Father,
now seated on high,
you have begun
your eternal reign
of justice and joy:
glory, glory,
glory, glory.

You're alive . . .

Graham Kendrick

CCL Licence No. _____

Let your living water flow over my soul.
Let your Holy Spirit come and take control
of ev'ry situation that has troubled my mind.
All my cares and burdens onto you I roll.

Jesus, Jesus,
Jesus.
Father, Father,
Father.
Spirit, Spirit
Spirit.

Come now, Holy Spirit, and take control.
Hold me in your loving arms and make me whole.
Wipe away all doubt and fear and take my pride.
Draw me to your love and keep me by your side.

Jesus . . .

Give your life to Jesus, let him fill your soul.
Let him take you in his arms and make you whole.
As you give your life to him he'll set you free.
You will live and reign with him eternally.

Jesus . . .

(Repeat verse 1)

John Watson

Copyright © 1986 Ampelos Music, Administered by CopyCare,
P.O. Box 77, Hailsham, BN27 3EF, U.K. Used by permission.

CCL Licence No. _____

Lord, you are so precious to me,
Lord, you are so precious to me,
and I love you,
yes, I love you
because you first loved me.

Lord, you are so gracious to me,
Lord, you are so gracious to me,
and I love you,
yes, I love you
because you first loved me.

Graham Kendrick

Majesty, worship his majesty;
unto Jesus be glory, honour and praise.
Majesty, kingdom authority
flows from his throne unto his own:
his anthem raise.

So exalt, lift up on high
the name of Jesus;
magnify, come glorify
Christ Jesus the King.
Majesty, worship his majesty,
Jesus who died, now glorified,
King of all kings.

Jack W. Hayford

My Lord, what love is this
that pays so dearly,
that I, the guilty one,
may go free!

Amazing love,
O what sacrifice,
the Son of God giv'n for me.
My debt he pays and my death he dies,
that I might live, that I might live.

And so they watched him die,
despised, rejected;
but oh, the blood he shed
flowed for me!

Amazing love . . .

And now this love of Christ
shall flow like rivers;
come wash your guilt away,
live again!

Amazing love . . .

Graham Kendrick

O Lord my God! When I in awesome wonder
consider all the works thy hand hath made,
I see the stars, I hear the mighty thunder,
thy power throughout the universe displayed:

*Then sings my soul, my Saviour God, to thee,
how great thou art! How great thou art!
Then sings my soul, my Saviour God, to thee,
how great thou art! How great thou art!*

When through the woods and forest glades I wander
and hear the birds sing sweetly in the trees;
when I look down from lofty mountain grandeur,
and hear the brook, and feel the gentle breeze;

Then sings my soul . . .

And when I think that God his Son not sparing,
sent him to die – I scarce can take it in.
That on the cross my burden gladly bearing,
he bled and died to take away my sin:

Then sings my soul . . .

Stuart K. Hine

When Christ shall come with shout of acclamation
and take me home – what joy shall fill my heart!
Then shall I bow in humble adoration
And there proclaim, my God, how great thou art!

Then sings my soul, my Saviour God, to thee,
how great thou art! How great thou art!
Then sings my soul, my Saviour God, to thee,
how great thou art! How great thou art!

O Lord, the clouds are gathering,
the fire of judgement burns,
how we have fallen!
O Lord, you stand appalled to see
your laws of love so scorned
and lives so broken.

Have mercy, Lord, (echo)
forgive us, Lord, (echo)
restore us, Lord,
revive your church again.
Let justice flow (echo)
like rivers (echo)
and righteousness like a never failing stream

O Lord, over the nations now
where is the dove of peace?
Her wings are broken.
O Lord, while precious children starve
the tools of war increase;
their bread is stolen.

Have mercy, Lord . . .

Graham Kendrick

O Lord, dark powers are poised to flood
our streets with hate and fear;
we must awaken!
O Lord, let love reclaim the lives
that sin would sweep away
and let your kingdom come.

Have mercy, Lord, (echo)
forgive us, Lord, (echo)
restore us, Lord,
revive your church again.
Let justice flow (echo)
like rivers (echo)
and righteousness like a never failing stream

Yet, O Lord, your glorious cross shall tower
triumphant in this land,
evil confounding.
Through the fire your suffering church display
the glories of her Christ:
praises resounding!

Have mercy, Lord . . .

Graham Kendrick

Open our eyes, Lord,
we want to see Jesus,
to reach out and touch him
and say that we love him.
Open our ears, Lord,
and help us to listen:
open our eyes, Lord,
we want to see Jesus!

Robert Cull

CCL Licence No. _____

Peace like a river,
love like a mountain,
the wind of your Spirit
is blowing ev'rywhere.
Joy like a fountain,
healing spring of life;
come, Holy Spirit,
let your fire fall.

John Watson

CCL Licence No. _____

Purify my heart,
let me be as gold
and precious silver.
Purify my heart,
let me be as gold,
pure gold.

Refiner's fire,
my heart's one desire
is to be holy,
set apart for you, Lord.
I choose to be holy,
set apart for you, my master,
ready to do your will.

Purify my heart,
cleanse me from within
and make me holy.
Purify my heart,
cleanse me from my sin,
deep within.

Refiner's fire . . .

Brian Doerksen

Rejoice in the Lord always,
and again I say, rejoice!
Rejoice in the Lord always,
and again I say, rejoice!
Rejoice, rejoice,
and again I say, rejoice!
Rejoice, rejoice,
and again I say, rejoice!

Evelyn Tarner

Shout for joy and sing
your praises to the King,
lift your voice and let
your hallelujahs ring;
come before his throne
to worship and adore,
Enter joyfully now
the presence of the Lord.

You are my creator,
you are my deliv'rer,
you are my redeemer,
you are Lord,
and you are my healer.
you are my provider,
you are now my shepherd,
And my guide,
Jesus, Lord and King,
I worship you.

David Fellingham

Spirit of the living God,
fall afresh on me;
Spirit of the living God,
fall afresh on me;
break me,
melt me,
mould me,
fill me.
Spirit of the living God,
fall afresh on me.

Such love, pure as the whitest snow;
such love weeps for the shame I know;
such love, paying the debt I owe;
O Jesus, such love.

Such love, stilling my restlessness;
such love, filling my emptiness;
such love, showing me holiness;
O Jesus, such love.

Such love springs from eternity;
such love, streaming through history;
such love, fountain of life to me;
O Jesus, such love.

Graham Kendrick

The Lord is marching out in splendour,
in awesome majesty he rides,
for truth, humility and justice,
his mighty army fills the skies.

O give thanks to the Lord
for his love endures,
O give thanks to the Lord
for his love endures,
O give thanks to the Lord
for his love endures for ever, for ever.

His army marches out with dancing,
for he has filled our hearts with joy.
Be glad the kingdom is advancing,
the love of God, our battle cry!

O give thanks . . .

Graham Kendrick

There is a Redeemer,
Jesus, God's own Son,
precious Lamb of God, Messiah,
Holy One.

Thank you, O my Father,
for giving us your Son,
and leaving your Spirit
till the work on earth is done.

Jesus, my Redeemer,
name above all names,
precious Lamb of God, Messiah,
O for sinners slain.

Thank you, O my Father . . .

When I stand in glory,
I will see his face,
and there I'll serve my King for ever,
in that holy place.

Thank you, O my Father . . .

Melody Green

Thou art worthy,
thou art worthy,
thou art worthy, O Lord.
Thou art worthy,
to receive glory.
glory and honour and power.

For thou hast created,
hast all things created,
for thou hast created all things.
And for thy pleasure
they are created;
thou art worthy, O Lord.

Thou art worthy,
thou art worthy,
thou art worthy, O Lamb.
Thou art worthy,
to receive glory.
And power at the Father's right hand.

Pauline Michael Mills

For thou hast redeemed us,
hast ransomed and cleaned us
by thy blood setting us free.
In white robes arrayed us,
kings and priests made us,
and we are reigning in thee.

Pauline Michael Mills

We are here to praise you,
lift our hearts and sing.
We are here to give you
the best that we can bring.

And it is our love rising from our hearts,
ev'rything within us cries:
'Abba Father.'
Help us now to give you pleasure and delight,
heart and mind and will that say:
'I love you Lord.'

Graham Kendrick

We shall stand
with our feet on the Rock.
Whatever men may say
we'll lift your name up high.
And we shall walk
through the darkest night;
setting our faces like flint
we'll walk into the light.

Lord, you have chosen me
for fruitfulness,
to be transformed into
your likeness.
I'm gonna fight on through
till I see you face to face.

We shall stand . . .

Lord, as your witnesses
you've appointed us,
and with your Holy Spirit
anointed us.
And so I'll fight on through
till I see you face to face.

We shall stand . . .

Graham Kendrick

We'll sing a new song of glorious triumph
for we see the government of God in our lives.
We'll sing a new song of glorious triumph
for we see the government of God in our lives.

He is crowned God of the whole world, crowned,
King of creation, crowned, ruling the nations now.
Yes he is crowned God of the whole world, crowned,
King of creation, crowned, ruling the nations now.

Diane Fung

When I look into your holiness,
when I gaze into your loveliness,
when all things that surround
become shadows in the light of you.
When I've found the joy
of reaching your heart,
when my will becomes
enthralled in your love,
when all things that surround
become shadows in the light of you:
I worship you, I worship you,
the reason I live is to worship you.
I worship you, I worship you,
the reason I live is to worship you.

Wayne & Cathy Perrin

CCL Licence No. _____

Acetate Masters Books 1-4
Complete Index

Abba Father 3
Ah Lord God 3
All hail the lamb 1
All heaven declares 2
All I once held dear 4
Alleluia, alleluia, give thanks 4
Almighty God 2
    Amazing love 2
And can it be 2
    Arms of love 2
As the deer 2
As we are gathered 3
Ascribe greatness to our God 1
Be bold, be strong 1
Be patient 2
Be Still 4
Behold the Lord 3
Bind us together 4
    Blessed be the Lord God Almighty 3
Blessed be the name of the Lord 4
By your side 2
Cast your burdens 3
Celebrate Jesus 3
Change my heart, O God 2
Colours of day 2
Come and see 4
    Come, Lord Jesus 4
Come on and Celebrate 1
Do not be afraid 2
Don't let my love grow cold 1
Down the mountain 4
Draw me closer 1
Fairest Lord Jesus 2
Faithful God 4
Faithful one 2
Father God I wonder 1
Father God we worship you 1
Father in heaven, how we love you 3
    Father me 3
Father of creation 1
Father, I come to you 4
Father, I place into your hands 2
Father, we adore you 4
Father, we adore you 1
Father, we love you 1
For I know my redeemer lives 3
For I'm building a people of power 3
For this purpose 4
    Fountain of life 4
    Freely, freely 3
From heaven you came 2
From the rising of the sun 4
Give thanks with a grateful heart 1
    Glorify your name 1
Glory 3
    Go tell everyone 1

God forgave my sin 3
God is good 2
God of glory 3
God's Spirit is in my heart 1
Great is the darkness 4
Great is the Lord 3
Great is thy faithfulness 3
Have you heard the raindrops 3
He brought me to his banqueting house 3
    He has made me glad 2
He has risen 2
He is exalted 1
He is Lord 1
He is Lord 3
    He is our fortress 4
    Heal our nation 4
    Higher Higher 3
    His banner over me is love 3
Hold me, Lord 2
Holiness unto the Lord 4
    Holy and anointed one 4
Holy Spirit, we welcome you 4
Hosanna 2
    Hosanna to the Son of David 1
    How great thou art 2
How lovely on the mountains 3
I am a new creation 4
I believe in Jesus 3
    I could sing of your love forever 3
I danced in the morning 1
I give you all the honour 3
I hear the sound of rustling 1
I just want to praise you 2
I lift my eyes up 2
I lift my hands 1
I love you, Lord 4
    I really want to worship you my Lord 1
I sing a simple song of love 2
    I stand in awe 3
I want to serve the purpose of God 4
I well seek your face 4
I will enter his gates 2
I will praise you all my life 1
    I will serve no foreign god 1
I will sing, I will sing 4
    I will sing your praises 1
    I worship you 3
I worship you, almighty God 4
I'm accepted 1
If I were a butterfly 3
    In my generation 4
In heavenly armour 2
Isn't he beautiful? 3
It is no longer I that liveth 3
It's your blood 1
    Jesus in our God 3

Jesus is Lord 4
Jesus is the name we honour 3
Jesus Love is very wonderful 1
Jesus put this song into our hearts 4
Jesus shall take the highest honour 3
Jesus, Jesus, holy and anointed one 4
Jesus, name above all names 1
Jesus, stand among us 2
Jesus, we celebrate your victory 2
Jesus, we enthrone you 4
   Jubilate Deo 1
Jubilate Everybody 1
   knowing you 4
Led like a lamb 2
Let there be love 1
   Let your glory fall 1
Let your living water flow 2
   Light up the fire 2
   Living water 2
Lord Jesus Christ 3
Lord of all hopefulness 4
   Lord of the dance 1
Lord the light of your love 1
Lord we long for you 4
Lord you are more precious 3
Lord, have mercy on us 1
Lord, I lift your name on high 3
Lord, you are so precious to me 2
Lord, you put a tongue into my mouth 1
Majesty 2
Make way 4
Meekness and majesty 4
More love, more power 4
   More precious than silver 3
Mothing shall separate us 1
My life is in you, Lord 1
My lips shall praise you 4
My Lord, what love is this 2
No one but you, Lord 1
No other name 1
O Father of the fatherless 3
   O faithful God 1
O give thanks 1
   O give thanks 2
O Lord our God 3
O Lord, my God 2
O Lord, the clouds are gathering 2
O Lord, your tenderness 3
One more step along the world I go 4
One thing I ask 3
One, two, three, Jesus loves me 3
Only by grace 1
   Only you 1
Open our eyes, Lord 2
Our confidence is in the Lord 4
   Our God reigns 3
Over the mountains and the sea 3
Peace like a river 2
Peace, perfect peace 4
Praise him on the trumpet 1
   Psalm 121 2

Purify my heart 2
   Refiner's fire 2
Reign in me 3
Rejoice in the Lord always 2
Rejoice! 3
   Restorer of my soul 4
Salvation belongs to our God 4
Seek ye first 3
   Shine Jesus shine 1
Shout for joy and sing 2
Show your power, O Lord 1
Spirit of the living God 2
Such love 2
Teach me to dance 4
Tell out my soul 1
Thank you, Jesus 1
Thank you, Lord, for this fine day 4
   The battle belongs to the Lord 2
   The butterfly song 3
The earth is the Lord's 4
The Lord is marching out 2
The Lord reigns 3
   The river is here 4
   The servant king 2
There is a redeemer 2
There is none like you 1
There is power in the name of Jesus 4
There's no one like you 3
This is the day 3
   This is your God 4
Thou art worthy 2
To be in your presence 1
   Unending love 4
   Water of life 3
We are here to praise you 2
We believe 4
We bring the sacrifice of praise 3
We declare your majesty 1
We have come into his house 4
We really want to thankyou 1
We shall stand 2
We want to see Jesus lifted high 3
   We will magnify 3
   We worship at your feet 4
We'll sing a new song 2
Welcome king of kings 1
When I feel the touch 4
When I look into your holiness 2
   White horse 2
Who put the colours in the rainbow? 4
Worthy, O worthy are you, Lord 3
   Worthy is the Lord 3
You are beautiful 3
You are crowned with many crowns 3
You are the King of glory 1
   You came from heaven to earth 3
You laid aside your majesty 1
You sat down 4
You shall go our with joy 4
   You're alive 2